THE

A TO Z

COLORING BOOK

THE A TO Z COLORING BOOK

BEAUTIFUL IMAGES TO CREATE COLORFUL LETTERING

SIRIUS

This edition published in 2021 by Sirius Publishing, a division of
Arcturus Publishing Limited,
26/27 Bickels Yard, 151–153 Bermondsey Street,
London SE1 3HA

ISBN: 978-1-3988-1021-1
CH008159NT
Supplier 29, Date 0321, Print run 11389

Printed in China

Created for children 10+

INTRODUCTION

Unleash your creativity and use the outlines in this book to produce a variety of embellished letters and make your own illustrated alphabet. From intricate designs that highlight animals, birds, and other objects which begin with that letter, to more graphic images, there is a wealth of different designs for you to choose from.

Before starting, it is worth thinking about the color schemes that you will use. You may want to give the images a peaceful and harmonious color combination. Conversely, bright and clashing tones can give an entirely different effect. Remember to think about the depth of tone as well – this can make the difference between a vivid, strong picture and a subtle, pale picture.

Pencil color is not as intense as paint, so it helps to add layers of color. When using darker shades, don't just apply a single layer of color. They will look better if you work over the same area several times to produce a greater intensity of color. For example, most black areas are either warm or cool in hue. To achieve this, apply a layer of black and then add another layer of deep brown (for warm tones) or dark blue (for cool tones) on top. If you want to make the black even more intense, color blue over brown over black, or brown over blue over black. Then, for the densest areas, add yet another layer of black.

For blue or red, add layers of different blues and reds to increase the intensity. Sometimes the addition of purple can also give a blue or a dark red more power in the composition. At other times, the top layer can be put on lightly to change the quality of the color a little.

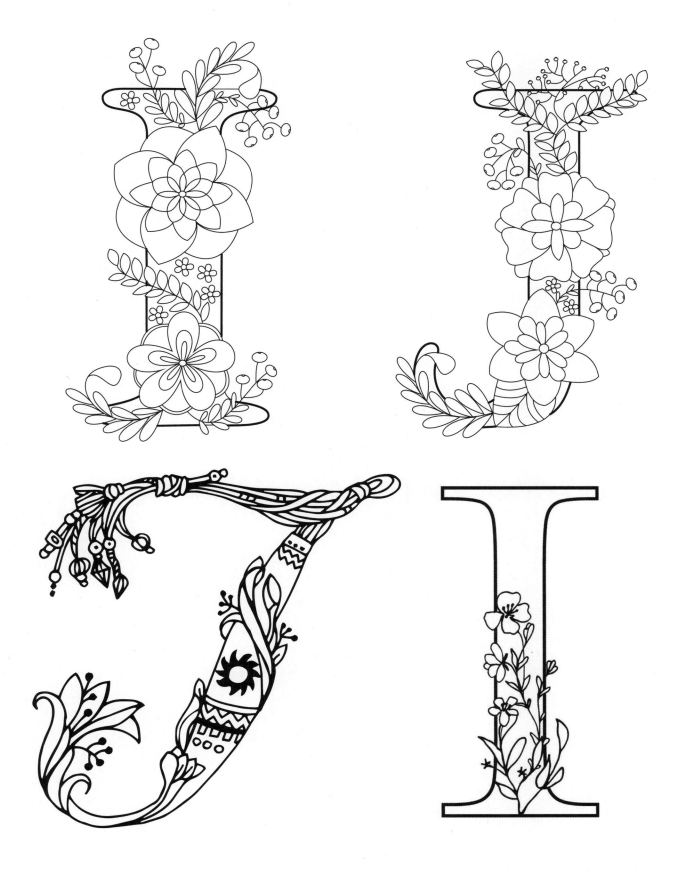

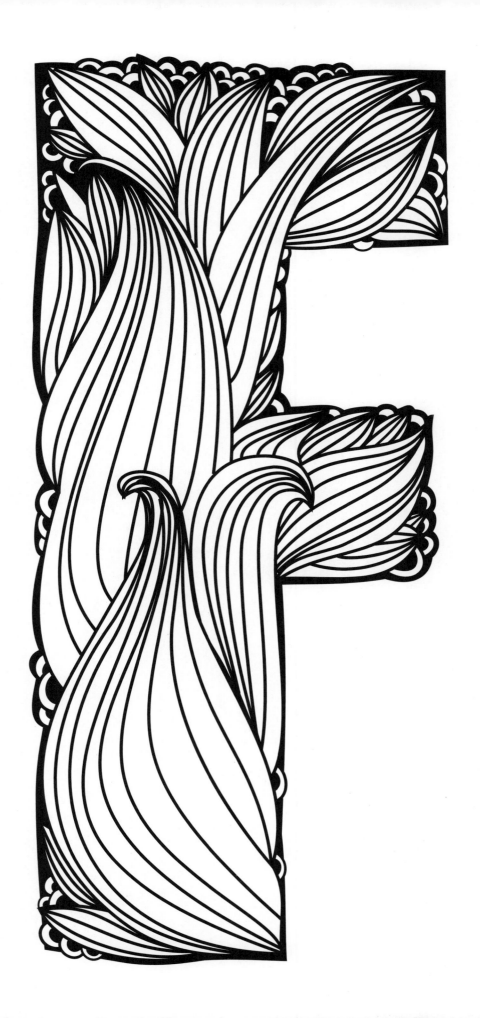

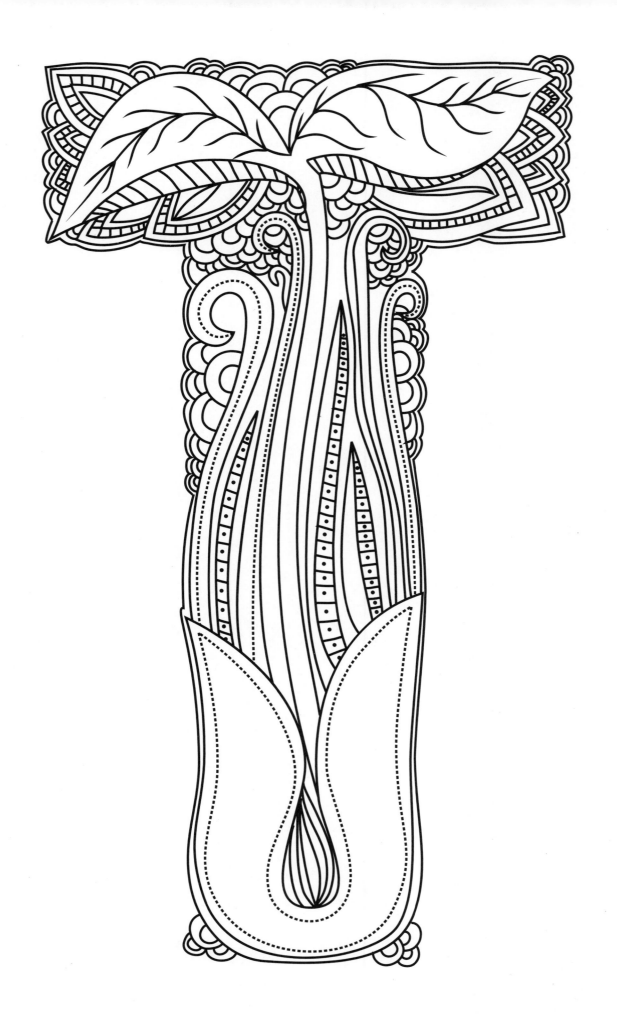